Where We Begin Again

Neha Patidar

AF658287

KKN Publication

KKN Publication

KKN Publication

(An imprint of KKN Media Group)

KKN Avenue, Ayachi Gram,
Bairiya, Muzaffarpur – 842003

Where We Begin Again

First Edition : February 2025

ISBN : 978-93-49314-53-5

Author : Neha Patidar

Instagram : nehapatidar_20_

KKN "Write & Learn" Initiative

This book is part of the KKN "Write & Learn" initiative, which aims to encourage new writers and promote the art of writing. The content presented is in its original form as submitted by the author(s) and may contain spelling, grammatical or structural errors. This book is intended solely for motivational purposes, and not as a representation of professional-quality publication. Readers are encouraged to appreciate and support the developmental journey of these authors, take inspiration for writing, and recognize that a society with more writers fosters creativity, diverse perspectives and intellectual growth.

Contents

Why Readers Should Read this Book

Where We Begin Again is for anyone who has ever faced heartbreak yet dared to love again. It's a story about overcoming fears, rediscovering oneself, and believing in the power of destiny. With relatable characters, heartfelt emotions, and moments that make you reflect on your own journey, this book is a reminder that love, no matter how complicated, is always worth the risk. If you enjoy emotionally rich stories that balance deep connections with personal growth, this book will resonate with you.

My Journey as an Author

Writing has always been my escape, a way to untangle emotions and explore the complexities of love, fate, and self-discovery. Where We Begin Again was born from my fascination with how love transforms us—how it challenges, heals, and reshapes our paths. Inspired by personal experiences and the stories around me, I wanted to craft a tale that reflects the beauty of second chances and the courage it takes to embrace love despite the past. This book is not just a romance; it's a journey of resilience, self-growth, and the magic of new beginnings.

The First Glimpse

A Moment Stolen

The world was loud,

But you moved through it softly.

I caught a glimpse of you,

And suddenly, the noise disappeared.

Eyes Like Sunlight

Your eyes-

Golden beams piercing the shadows.

A fleeting glance,

And I was undone.

The Room Went Quiet

In a room full of strangers,

You stood out like a flame.

The moment our eyes met,

Time forgot to move.

A Breath Held

I didn’t know your name,

But I knew your presence.

A quiet pull,

Like gravity finding its match.

The First Smile

It wasn't just a smile;

It was a doorway,

And I was invited to step through.

Threads of Fate

I don't believe in destiny,

But when I saw you,

I felt the strings of the universe

Tie me to you.

A Passing Shadow

You walked by,

A fleeting shadow in my world.

But in your wake,

You left my heart racing.

Something Familiar

I'd never met you before,

Yet you felt like a memory.

A home I hadn't found until now.

A Single Glance

It was a single glance,

A brief spark in the darkness.

But that spark ignited

An entire universe in me.

The Color of You

In a grayscale world,

You were color.

Vivid, vibrant, alive.

I couldn't look away.

A Quiet Hello

Your hello was quiet,

But it echoed in my chest,

A whisper that refused to fade.

The First Brush

Our hands brushed,

A touch so light it could have been forgotten.

But it lingered,

A secret shared between my skin and yours.

Like the Sunrise

You rose in my world

Like the first light of dawn—

Gentle, breathtaking, inevitable.

The Beginning

There was no warning,

No sign,

Just you,

And a heart that suddenly

Forgot how to beat.

Unwritten Stories

In your eyes,
I saw stories untold,
Worlds unexplored,
And I wanted to know them all.

A Star Fell

A star fell from the sky that night,
And it landed in you.
Your glow lit up my life.

Before Words

We didn't need words;

The silence spoke for us.

A language only our hearts could understand.

The First Thread

The thread began

With a glance,

And I knew it wouldn't break.

The Curve of Your Smile

It was just a curve,

But it bent my entire world.

A Stranger No More

You were a stranger

Until you weren't.

One moment changed everything.

A Breath Away

You passed me by,
A breath of air,
And suddenly, I was awake.

The First Beat

The world was quiet,
Until I heard your laugh.
It became the rhythm
I didn't know I was missing.

Time Stood Still

It wasn't just your face;
It was the way time paused
To admire you, too.

A Window to Forever

Your eyes held a promise,
A window to something endless.
I stepped closer,
Afraid of falling,
Yet desperate to dive.

Everything Changed

It was just a second,

A fleeting instant.

But in that moment,

Everything changed.

A Name I Don't Know

I don't know your name,

But I feel it in my chest,

A melody waiting to be sung.

A Heart Unlocked

Your glance was a key,
And before I knew it,
You'd unlocked the door
I kept so tightly closed.

Electric

The air crackled when you appeared,
An unspoken energy between us.
I felt it in my bones,
And I knew—
You were something more.

A Stranger's Magic

You were a stranger,

But your presence felt magical.

A story waiting to unfold.

The Beginning of Us

It was nothing,

And it was everything.

A glance, a moment,

The beginning of us.

THE BEGINNING

The First Spark

It wasn't fire,

But a flicker,

A gentle warmth

That grew with every glance.

A New Dawn

Love arrived quietly,

Like the first light of morning.

I didn't see it coming,

But I felt its glow.

Your Smile

It wasn't just a curve-

It was an invitation,

A doorway to a world

I longed to explore.

The Meeting

We didn't plan for this,

But the universe must have.

Two hearts colliding,

A story waiting to begin.

Like Rain

Love came softly,

Like a drizzle on a summer day.

Unnoticed at first,

But soon,

It drenched me completely.

The Language of Us

Before we spoke,

Our eyes exchanged

A language only hearts could understand.

In That Moment

A glance, a touch,

A laugh shared between us—

In that moment,

The world shifted.

First Steps

Love doesn't leap;

It tiptoes in,

One heartbeat at a time.

Magnetic Pull

Your presence drew me closer,
A pull I couldn't resist.
Gravity had nothing
On the force of us.

An Unexpected Start

I didn't know I was searching
Until I found you.
Love began
When I least expected it.

A Whisper

Your voice was a whisper,
Soft and inviting.
It echoed in my chest,
Refusing to leave.

The Color of You

You brought color to my world,
Blues, reds, and golds—
A canvas I never knew
Needed painting.

The First Hello

Your hello
Was a spark in the dark,
A quiet promise
Of something beautiful to come.

The Bridge Between

Each word we spoke
Built a bridge
Between your world and mine.
Now I walk it daily.

A Quiet Start

Love doesn't always shout.

Sometimes,

It's the quiet moments

That mean the most.

The Way You Looked at Me

It wasn't just a look;

It was a revelation.

In your eyes,

I saw the beginning of forever.

Like a Song

You were a melody,
And I was a listener,
Entranced by every note.

A Garden of Words

Our conversations were seeds,
Planting a garden
Of trust, laughter, and dreams.

Something New

I had seen the stars before,

But they shone differently

The night I met you.

A Gentle Start

Like a breeze through the trees,

Your presence moved me,

Subtle but profound.

The First Chapter

This is where it began—

Not with fireworks,

But with a quiet certainty

That you were meant for me.

Between the Lines

Every pause between our words

Felt like a secret waiting to be shared.

The Bloom

Our love began as a bud,

Fragile and new.

But with time,

It blossomed into something beautiful.

Your Laughter

Your laugh was a melody,

And I found myself humming it,

Long after you were gone.

Like Fireflies

Love began

In the fleeting moments—

A glance, a smile,

A touch that lingered.

The Dance of Us

We didn't rush;

We swayed,

Letting love find its rhythm

Between us.

A Candle's Glow

Love didn't arrive as a flame,
But as a candle's glow—
Gentle, steady,
Lighting the way.

Like a Secret

Love was a secret
The universe whispered
Into my heart
The day I met you.

A Heart Awake

I didn't know my heart was asleep

Until your love woke it up,

Beating in a rhythm

I never knew was missing.

The Start of Forever

This isn't just a moment;

It's the beginning of eternity.

For in your eyes,

I've found my home.

FALLING IN LOVE

A Soft Landing

I didn't fall—

I drifted into you,

A gentle descent

Into a love I didn't know

I was searching for.

Piece by Piece

Your laugh,

Your touch,

The way you say my name—

Each piece of you

Fits perfectly into my world.

Your Voice

Your voice is a melody,
A song my heart hums
Even in the quiet.

The Dance of Us

We move together,
Not in a rush,
But in a rhythm
That feels eternal.

A Love Unexpected

I wasn't looking for love,

But it found me anyway—

Soft and persistent,

In the shape of you.

Between Heartbeats

Somewhere between my heartbeats,

I found you.

And now,

You're the reason they continue.

A World in Your Eyes

Your eyes hold galaxies,

And I want to explore

Every star,

Every light

That makes you shine.

The Way You See Me

When you look at me,

I feel seen—

Not just for who I am,

But for who I could be.

Safe Harbor

Your arms are a harbor,
A place where my storms
Turn into calm.

Slow Bloom

Our love isn't hurried;
It's a flower that blooms slowly,
Unfolding with care
And endless beauty.

Quiet Magic

Love isn't always loud.
Sometimes it's in the quiet—
The way your hand finds mine
Without a word.

The Thread

We're tied together,
Not by chance,
But by a thread
The universe carefully wove.

Becoming Us

I was me,

You were you,

But now we're something more—

A beautiful us.

The Sweetness of You

Falling for you

Is like tasting honey

For the first time—

Golden, sweet,

And unforgettable.

Morning Light

Your love is like the morning—
A gentle light
That wakes me up
To something beautiful.

Like Breathing

Loving you feels natural,
Like breathing,
Like existing.

The First Touch

Your touch was electricity,
Not shocking,
But warm—
A spark I never knew I needed.

A New Chapter

Every moment with you
Feels like writing a story,
One I never want to end.

A Love That Grows

With every word,
With every laugh,
With every glance,
I fall for you a little more.

Starlit Nights

Under the stars,
I see eternity in your eyes.
And I wonder—
Was the universe made for us?

In Your Arms

The world is chaotic,

But in your arms,

Everything falls into place.

Unfolding Love

You're not just someone I love—

You're a mystery I want to unravel,

One layer at a time.

Love's Quiet Whisper

Love didn't shout.

It whispered softly

Every time you smiled,

And I heard it loud and clear.

The Fire Within

Your love isn't a blaze;

It's a steady flame,

Warming the coldest corners

Of my heart.

A Safe Place

You're my refuge,

A home I didn't know

I was missing.

In Every Breath

I breathe you in

Like air—

Necessary,

Unseen,

And vital.

A Gentle Fall

Falling for you

Isn't a rush—

It's a slow, beautiful descent

Into the softest place

I've ever known.

Your Love is a River

Your love flows through me,

Steady and unyielding.

I let it carry me,

And I never want to reach the shore.

The Language of Us

Your touch speaks volumes,

Your glance is poetry,

And together,

We've created a language of love.

Complete in You

I wasn't incomplete,

But with you,

I feel whole.

CHALLENGES

Fractures

We didn't break all at once,

But slowly,

Like cracks spreading in glass—

Fragile,

And impossible to repair.

The Silence Between Us

Your silence speaks louder now,

A wall between us,

Built brick by brick

With unsaid words.

Distant Shores

We stand on the same shore,

But the tides have pulled us apart.

The waves whisper of what we once were.

Storms of Us

Love isn't always gentle;

Sometimes it's a storm,

Tearing through our hearts,

Leaving us to rebuild.

The Weight of Words

Your words once lifted me,

But now they weigh me down.

How did love become so heavy?

A House Divided

Our love was a home,

But now it's just walls.

Where did the warmth go?

Lost in Translation

We speak the same language,

But somehow,

Our hearts are lost in translation.

Shadows of Doubt

The shadows of doubt

Creep between us,

Turning love's light

Into something dim.

The Distance in Your Eyes

I look into your eyes

And see a distance

I can't seem to close.

What We Don't Say

It's not the arguments that hurt—

It's the things we don't say,

The silences that grow

Like weeds between us.

The Fragility of Us

We are glass,
Beautiful but fragile.
One wrong move,
And we shatter.

The Edge of Goodbye

We stand on the edge,
Neither moving closer
Nor walking away.
How long can we teeter like this?

A Love Tested

Love is easy
Until it's tested.
Now, every word feels like a question
We can't answer.

The Blame Game

Your words are arrows,
Mine are shields.
When did we forget
How to love without fighting?

A Tired Heart

My heart is tired—

Not of loving you,

But of fighting to be loved back.

The Pieces We Broke

We broke something,

And no amount of glue

Can make it whole again.

When Love Hurts

Love wasn't supposed to hurt,

But here we are,

Carrying wounds

We gave each other.

The Quiet Drift

We didn't notice it at first—

The quiet drift

That pulled us apart.

A Love Misaligned

We were perfect pieces,

But somehow,

We no longer fit.

Ghosts of Us

Our love is haunted

By the ghosts of what we used to be.

How do we exorcise them?

Apologies Left Unsaid

I want to say I'm sorry,
But the words catch in my throat.
Why is it so hard
To heal what we've broken?

The Things We Carry

We carry so much—
The weight of our past,
The burden of our fears.
How can love survive beneath it all?

Cracks in the Foundation

The foundation of us

Is cracked,

And I don't know

If it can hold us anymore.

Love in the Dark

We've turned off the light,

And now we fumble

To find each other in the dark.

Broken Promises

We promised forever,

But forever feels fragile now—

A promise we're struggling to keep.

The Fear of Losing You

I fear losing you,

But the truth is,

I feel like I already have.

The Rift Between Us

There's a rift between us,

Growing wider each day.

How do we bridge a gap

We can't even name?

Love on Hold

Our love is on pause,

Waiting for the moment

We find the strength

To press play again.

Fighting for Us

Love isn't easy,

But it's worth the fight.

I just hope

We're both still fighting.

The Question of Us

Are we meant to be?

Or are we holding on

To something that no longer exists?

I don't know the answer,

But I can't let go.

HEALING AND REDISCOVERY

The First Step

Healing starts small-

A touch, a word,

A moment of forgiveness

Shared between us.

Like Spring

Our love was frozen,

But now it thaws.

Beneath the surface,

New life begins to grow.

Stitch by Stitch

Our hearts were torn,

But with patience and care,

We sew them back together.

Learning to Trust Again

Trust isn't given—

It's rebuilt,

One promise kept,

One fear soothed.

A New Beginning

This isn't where we started,

But it's a beginning nonetheless.

Love can bloom

Even in unexpected places.

Forgiveness is a Gift

It isn't easy,

But forgiveness is the bridge

We must walk

To find each other again.

The Light Returns

The darkness came,

But it didn't stay.

Now, I see the light

In your eyes again.

Letting Go

The past holds no power

When we choose to let it go,

Makin

g space for something new.

Hands Together

Your hand in mine

Is a quiet reminder—

We are stronger together

Than apart.

The Garden of Us

We've pulled the weeds,

Planted new seeds.

Our love is a garden

Ready to bloom again.

Love's Second Chance

They say love can't be reborn,
But here we are,
Writing a new chapter
With the same hearts.

A New Rhythm

We've learned a new rhythm,
One that beats gently,
Softly guiding us forward.

Healing Touch

Your touch was once familiar,

But now it feels new-

A balm to the wounds

We've both carried.

Rebuilding the Bridge

The bridge was broken,

But stone by stone,

We've built a path

Back to each other.

The Strength in Us

Our love isn't fragile anymore;
It's stronger,
Forged in the fire
Of what we've overcome.

Soft Apologies

We whispered apologies,
Soft and sincere.
They became the foundation
For something stronger.

A Gentle Rediscovery

I'm learning you again,

Each smile, each glance—

A rediscovery

Of the beauty I first fell for.

The Weight is Gone

We carried so much,

But now the weight is gone.

Love feels light again.

A Quiet Resolve

We don't need fireworks,

Only the quiet resolve

To choose each other every day.

The Power of Patience

Healing isn't quick,

But with patience,

Love finds its way back

To where it belongs.

A Love Renewed

Our love isn't what it was—

It's deeper,

Stronger,

More beautiful than before.

Through the Cracks

Even broken things

Can hold beauty.

Through the cracks of us,

Light shines.

A Soft Beginning

This isn't an end,
But a soft beginning—
A chance to love each other
Better than before.

Scars and Stories

Our scars are stories,
Not of pain,
But of resilience,
Of a love that refused to fade.

Choosing Us Again

Every day,

We choose us again,

Turning pain into a memory,

And love into forever.

The Beauty of Healing

Healing isn't perfect,

But it's beautiful—

A journey we take

Hand in hand.

Learning to Laugh Again

Your laugh feels lighter now,

And so does mine.

We've found joy

In the simple things again.

Rediscovering You

You're still the same,

But somehow new.

Each moment with you

Feels like the first.

The Song Returns

Our love was a song

Once lost to silence.

But now,

The music plays again.

Love After the Storm

The storm passed,

And we're still standing.

Our love is the rainbow,

Proof that beauty

Can follow the darkest skies.

ETERNITY

Forever Yours

Time has no power here,
For my heart beats for you
In every moment,
Forever and always.

Timeless Flame

The years may pass,
But our love remains,
A flame untouched
By the winds of time.

Endless Path

With you,

There's no end-

Only a path that stretches

Beyond the horizon.

Beyond the Stars

If love had a limit,

It would never reach the stars.

But ours goes farther still—

An infinite expanse.

A Love That Lasts

They say nothing lasts forever,
But here we stand,
Proving eternity wrong
With every heartbeat.

Through Lifetimes

If there are other lives,
I will find you in each,
For our souls are bound
Beyond this one.

The Echo of Us

Even when we're gone,

The world will remember—

The echo of our love

Will never fade.

Like the Ocean

Our love is like the sea,

Endless, powerful,

Carving eternity

Into the shores of our hearts.

The Golden Thread

We are stitched together
By a golden thread,
Unbroken,
Stretching into forever.

Eternal Spring

With you,
Every day feels like spring,
A love blooming endlessly
Through every season.

Love's Horizon

The horizon ends,

But our love does not—

It reaches places

Even the sun cannot touch.

A Circle Complete

Our love is a circle—

No beginning,

No end,

Just infinite devotion.

Timeless Dance

We dance through the years,

Stepping to a rhythm

That time cannot change.

Beyond Forever

Forever isn't long enough

For what I feel for you.

Our love stretches

Beyond even that.

Unending Story

Ours is a story
Without a final chapter-
An eternal tale
Written in the stars.

The Promise of Always

In your eyes,
I see the promise of always,
A love that defies
Time and space.

Carved in Time

If time is a river,

Our love is the stone—

Unmoving,

Enduring every current.

The Forever Flame

Through storms and shadows,

Our love burns bright—

An eternal flame

That cannot be snuffed out.

The Bridge of Us

We've built a bridge,

Not to cross oceans,

But to span eternity itself.

An Infinite Sky

Your love is the sky-

Endless,

And I'm content

To soar in it forever.

Beyond the Veil

Even when this life ends,

I know we'll meet again,

For love like ours

Cannot be confined by mortality.

Anchored in Love

Our love is an anchor,

Holding steady

Through the tides of time.

Eternal Flame

You are my forever-
The light that never dims,
The warmth that never fades.

The Language of Always

There's no word for it—
The way my heart speaks to yours,
In a language that says,
"Always."

Celestial Bond

We are more than flesh and bone—

We are stars bound together,

Shining across the ages.

The Timeless Whisper

Even in silence,

Your love whispers to me,

A quiet promise

That eternity is ours.

Endless Road

There's no final destination

For love like ours—

Only an endless road

We walk together.

The Echo of Forever

Our love echoes

Through every moment,

A song that never ends.

Boundless Love

There are no edges here—
Just love stretching outward,
Boundless and eternal.

Eternity's Embrace

If time is the ocean,
Then we are its waves,
Forever moving,
Forever entwined.